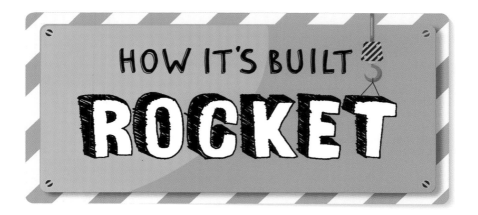

HOW IT'S BUILT

ROCKET

by Elise Wallace

Illustrations by Richard Watson

Children's Press®
An imprint of Scholastic Inc.

Thanks to Dr. Ron Barrett-Gonzalez, Professor of Aerospace Engineering, University of Kansas, for his role as content consultant for this book.

Thanks to Donna Lowich, Senior Information Specialist at the Christopher & Dana Reeve Foundation, for her insights into the daily lives of people who use wheelchairs.

Library of Congress Cataloging-in-Publication Data
Names: Wallace, Elise, author. | Watson, Richard, 1980– illustrator.
Title: How it's built. Rocket / by Elise Wallace; illustrated by Richard Watson.
Other titles: Rocket
Description: First edition. | New York, NY: Children's Press, an imprint of Scholastic Inc.,
    2022. | Includes index. | Audience: Ages 5–7 | Audience: Grades K–1 | Summary: "Narrative
    nonfiction with fictional characters who visit various work sites to find out how rockets are built.
    Full-color illustrations and photographs throughout"—Provided by publisher.
Identifiers: LCCN 2021029559 (print) | LCCN 2021029560 (ebook) | ISBN 9781338800203 (library binding) |
    ISBN 9781338800210 (paperback) | ISBN 9781338800241 (ebk)
Subjects: LCSH: Rockets (Aeronautics)—Design and construction—Juvenile literature. | BISAC: JUVENILE
    NONFICTION/Technology/How Things Work–Are Made
Classification: LCC TL782.5 .W35 2022 (print) | LCC TL782.5 (ebook) | DDC 621.43/56—dc23
LC record available at https://lccn.loc.gov/2021029559
LC ebook record available at https://lccn.loc.gov/2021029560

10 9 8 7 6 5 4 3 2 1   22 23 24 25 26

Printed in the U.S.A.   113
First edition, 2022

Series produced by Spooky Cheetah Press
Book design by Maria Bergós, Book & Look
Page design by Kathleen Petelinsek, The Design Lab

Photos ©: cover: SpaceX/NASA; back cover: SpaceX/Getty Images; 5 top, bottom left: NASA; 5 bottom right: Official SpaceX Photos/Flickr; 6 left: Detlev van Ravenswaay/Science Source; 6 right: NASA/Science Source; 7 left: NASA; 7 right: Joe Davila/U.S. Air Force; 8–9: Glenn Benson/NASA; 10 right: Official SpaceX Photos/Flickr; 11 left: Randy Beaudoin/NASA/Flickr; 11 right: SpaceX/Flickr; 12–13: Official SpaceX Photos/Flickr; 14 left: NASA/Getty Images; 14 right: Teslarati/SpaceX/Flickr; 15 left: NASA; 15 right: Steve Jurvetson/Flickr; 16–17: Official SpaceX Photos/Flickr; 18 left: NASA; 18 right: Official SpaceX Photos/Flickr; 19 left: Steve Jurvetson/Flickr; 20–21: NASA/Alamy Images; 22 left: Joe Skipper/Reuters/Alamy Images; 22 right: NASA/eyevine/Redux; 23 left: Jim Grossmann/NASA; 23 right: 2CMSteve Nesius/Reuters/Alamy Images; 24–25: SpaceX/NASA; 24 inset: NOAA/Getty Images; 26–27: Paul Hennessy/SOPA Images/LightRocket/Getty Images; 28 top left: Tony Landis/NASA; 28 top right: Doug Stoffer/MSFC/NASA; 28 bottom: Official SpaceX Photos/Flickr; 29 top left: Boeing/NASA; 29 top right: RGB Ventures/SuperStock/Alamy Images; 29 bottom: Glenn Benson/NASA; 30 top left: SpaceX/UPI/Shutterstock; 30 top right: NASA; 30 bottom: Mack Crawford/NASA; 31 top left: Detlev van Ravenswaay/Science Source; 31 right: Courtesy of Blue Origin; 31 bottom left: Michal Wachucik/AFP/Getty Images.

All other photos © Shutterstock.

TABLE OF CONTENTS

MEET THE JUNIOR ENGINEERS CLUB

Sofia

Lucas

Kai

Nisha

Jacob

Zoe

These six friends love learning about
how things are built! This is their workshop.

Lucas and Sofia found out how rockets are built.
Now they are sharing what they learned!

Most big rockets take from one to five years to build. Some take more than 10 years!

PROJECTS
HOUSE
CAR
BRIDGE
SKYSCRAPER
ROCKET
SAILBOAT

HOW TO BUILD A WATER-POWERED ROCKET

Hi! I'm Lucas. This is my sister Sofia. We took a trip to a rocket factory, where we met Mae and Tom. They're rocket engineers! That means they design rockets and the parts that go in them.

Rockets are vehicles. They are used to launch people and things into space. Mae and Tom showed us how rockets have changed over time.

R-7 (1957—present)
The R-7 was the first rocket to launch a satellite into space. A satellite is a small object that travels around a larger object, like a moon or a planet. R-7 rockets are still used today.

Saturn V (1967—1973)
The Saturn V was a huge rocket. It was more than 350 feet (107 meters) tall! The Saturn V was built to launch people to the moon. It also carried a lunar rover. That is a vehicle the astronauts used to drive on the moon.

US Space Shuttle (1981–2011)
This spacecraft was unique! It had wings and landing gear. It launched into space like a rocket and landed like a plane when it returned to Earth.

Delta IV Heavy (2014–present)
This rocket is used when a lot of weight needs to be carried into space. The Delta IV Heavy is the world's largest working rocket.

If you could, where would you go in a rocket?

I would love to walk on the moon!

Then Mae and Tom told us all about the Falcon 9 rocket, which was due to launch the next day. Unlike many rockets, the Falcon 9 is reusable. Its parts can be flown again and again.

Height: 230 ft. (70 m), taller than a 20-story building.

Weight: 1,210,457 pounds (549,054 kilograms), more than 85 elephants.

NASA (the National Aeronautics and Space Administration) is in charge of the US space program. Until 2000, NASA built all the American rockets used in space. Today, private companies build rockets, too. Falcon 9 is built by a private company.

Some rockets cost billions of dollars!

Yes, but rockets that have reusable parts can be less expensive to build.

Next, Sofia and I learned all about rocket design. Tom told us that rockets have four main systems.

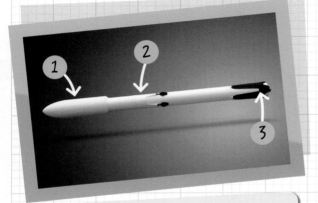

The **structural system** is the frame of the rocket. It is made of strong and lightweight materials. The frame has a nose cone (1), a body (2), and fins (3).

The **propulsion system** includes the engines, the fuel, and the parts to get the fuel to the engines. The propulsion system takes up most of the space in the rocket.

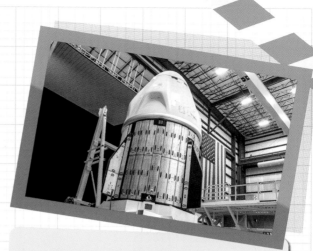

The **payload system** helps carefully hold and protect the cargo on the bumpy ride to space. Astronauts and satellites are both examples of rocket cargo.

The **guidance, navigation, and control system** is like the brains of the rocket. It senses where the rocket is and figures out where it should go. Then it sends control signals to the rocket motor controllers to move the rocket.

Rockets are complex. They have millions of parts!

11

Tom and Mae showed us how a rocket's frame is put together. The frame is made of thin metal sheets that are curved to fit the rocket's design. The metal sheets are then welded—or joined using heat.

Giant presses are used to curve a rocket's metal panels. The presses turn large metal sheets into circular tubes.

Thin metal gives the Falcon 9 a lighter structure.

And a rocket structure that weighs less is easier to launch into space!

Then came our favorite part of the tour. We got to see the Falcon 9's propulsion system up close! Tom and Mae told us about the main parts of this system and how a rocket engine works.

Octaweb
The rocket has nine first-stage engines. They are stored in the octaweb. The octaweb is built by welding sheet metal.

First-Stage Engines
These are the engines that launch the rocket. They break away from the rocket once it enters space. Then they fall back to Earth.

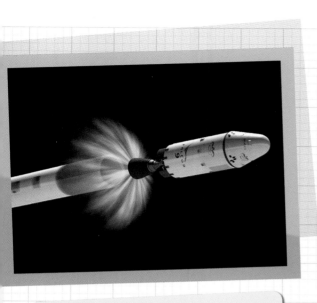

Second-Stage Engine
This engine does not fire until the rocket is in space. It powers the rocket to its final speed and altitude.

Tanks
Fuel is stored in huge metal tanks. The Falcon 9 uses kerosene and liquid oxygen fuels. They are stored in separate tanks.

First-stage engines are heavy.

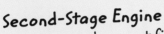

Oh, I get it! When they break away, the rocket's load is much lighter.

15

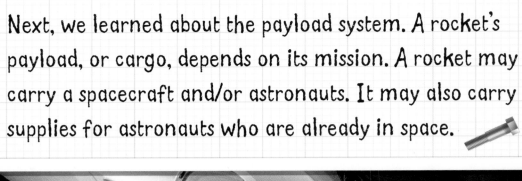

Next, we learned about the payload system. A rocket's payload, or cargo, depends on its mission. A rocket may carry a spacecraft and/or astronauts. It may also carry supplies for astronauts who are already in space.

Space suits protect astronauts from super-cold temperatures and radiation from the sun.

When astronauts are a rocket's "payload," they travel in a crew module. Crew modules must pass many tests to make sure that astronauts will be safe as they travel through space.

And also from super-fast speeds!

A rocket's guidance, navigation, and control system is very important. It guides the rocket through each stage of its journey. Here are some parts of this system that we learned about!

Engineers use **Global Positioning System (GPS)** satellites to monitor the weather. That's how they decide if the weather is right for a launch. GPS is also used to track rockets as they travel through space.

Onboard computers show when a rocket speeds up or slows down. They monitor a rocket's position in space and the direction it is pointed in. Onboard computers help rockets have safe and successful missions.

A rocket's **nozzles** can move from side to side. They help guide the rocket. Their movement helps the rocket change direction.

Rockets also have a communication system.

Yes! It lets astronauts send videos from space!

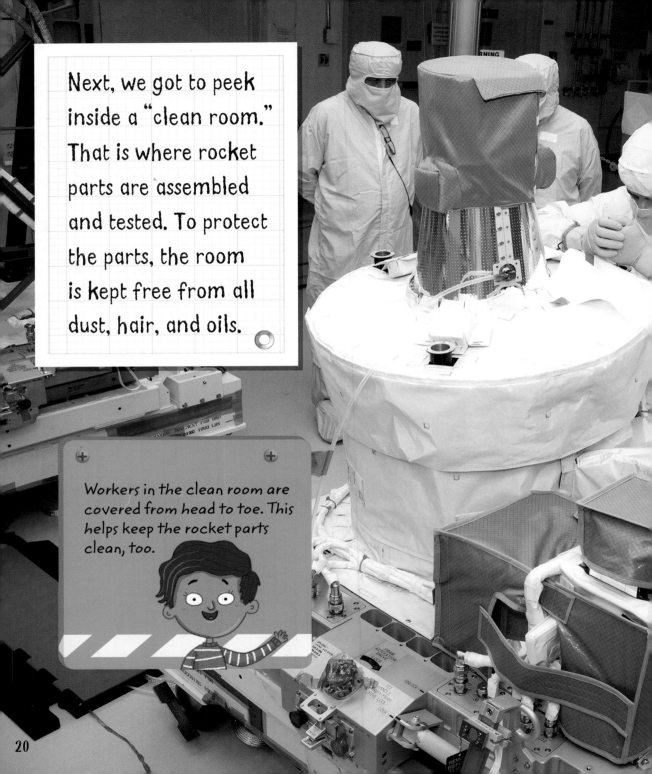

Next, we got to peek inside a "clean room." That is where rocket parts are assembled and tested. To protect the parts, the room is kept free from all dust, hair, and oils.

Workers in the clean room are covered from head to toe. This helps keep the rocket parts clean, too.

It was time to start preparing for the launch!
Sofia and I learned that before a Falcon 9
rocket takes flight, many things must happen.

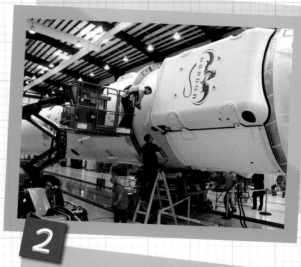

1

On the Road
Rocket parts are huge.
Trucks are used to transport
them to the launch site,
such as Cape Canaveral in
Florida. Sometimes trains
and barges are used as well.

2

Assembly Required
Once the rocket parts
reach their destination,
they are put together.

3

To the Launchpad

A special vehicle is used to transport the rocket to the launchpad. That is the exact spot from which it will take off. This vehicle raises the rocket from the ground to its launch position.

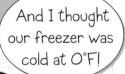

4

Fuel Up

The rocket's tanks are filled with kerosene and liquid oxygen a few hours before launch time.

Liquid oxygen must be kept very cold.

That's right: -340°F.

And I thought our freezer was cold at 0°F!

23

The next day, we met Tom and Mae at the launch site. It was almost time for liftoff. Tom and Mae described what was about to happen. The fuel in the rocket's engine would burn, make big flames, and launch the rocket into the air!

The weather has to be just right for a rocket launch. If it is rainy, windy, or even too cold or cloudy, the launch will be moved to another day.

Finally, the rocket was ready to launch. Mae and Tom took Sofia and me to the observation deck. The rest of the club was waiting there. The junior engineers had fulfilled their mission. They had learned how rockets are built! It was time to celebrate.

MACHINERY AND TOOLS FOR BUILDING A ROCKET

Software
Computer programs are key rocket-building tools. Different programs are used to design and test rocket parts.

Friction Stir Welder
Friction is when one object rubs another and causes heat. This tool uses the heat from friction to join metal panels.

Tool for Forming Composite Parts
A composite part is one that is made from two or more materials. For example, many rocket parts are made of carbon fiber combined with another material. Composite parts are made by special machines, like the one at left.

Dome Weld Tool
Giant rockets need giant tools! This tool is used to weld the domes of rocket tanks.

X-Ray Machine

X-Ray Machines
Engineers want to make sure rockets are superstrong. They use X-ray machines to look closely at rocket parts. They check for defects.

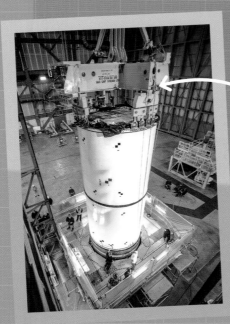

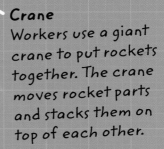

Crane
Workers use a giant crane to put rockets together. The crane moves rocket parts and stacks them on top of each other.

THE FUTURE OF ROCKETS

Engineers are developing rockets that can fly farther
and carry heavier payloads than ever before!

Starship SN15
The Starship SN15 may become
the world's most powerful rocket.
Engineers have designed it to
take people to Mars!

Space Launch System
This NASA rocket is a giant. It is taller
than the Statue of Liberty! The SLS
will take astronauts to the moon in
the near future.

Vulcan Centaur
The Vulcan Centaur
will come in different
shapes and sizes. Some
Vulcan Centaur rockets
will have two engines.
Some will have six, for
more power!

Neutron

Like the Falcon 9, the Neutron will be a reusable rocket. It will be used to build satellite constellations. Those are groups of satellites that work together in space.

New Glenn

The New Glenn's payload is extra big. It is much larger than any rocket of its kind. That means the New Glenn will have more room to store satellites, astronauts, and other cargo.

Prime

The Prime will have a unique engine. It will be made using a special 3D printer. The printer is able to follow an engineer's design to "print" the rocket engine in a single piece!

INDEX

ABOUT THE AUTHOR

Elise Wallace is an author and editor who lives in California and has traveled all over the world. She hopes to travel to space one day!